IAN LENDLER

One Day a Dot

ILLUSTRATED BY
SHELLI PAROLINE
& BRADEN LAMB

:01

First Second
New York

To Theo and Dylan,
my always-evolving little apes.

—I.L.

First Second

Text copyright © 2018 by Ian Lendler
Illustrations copyright © 2018 by Shelli Paroline and Braden Lamb

Published by First Second
First Second is an imprint of Roaring Brook Press, a division of Holtzbrinck
Publishing Holdings Limited Partnership
175 Fifth Avenue, New York, New York 10010

Library of Congress Control Number: 2017946152

ISBN 978-1-62672-244-6

Our books may be purchased in bulk for promotional, educational, or business use. Please
contact your local bookseller or the Macmillan Corporate and
Premium Sales Department at (800) 221-7945 ext. 5442 or by e-mail at
MacmillanSpecialMarkets@macmillan.com.

First edition, 2018

Book design by Danielle Ceccolini
Printed in China by RR Donnelley Asia Printing Solutions Ltd.,
Dongguan City, Guangdong Province
1 3 5 7 9 10 8 6 4 2

Penciled and inked with a Sumi Dry Brush in Clip Studio Paint.
Colored in Photoshop.

One day a dot appeared.

And it was so excited
to be there

that it burst.

This made beautiful
new dots that were so
attractive that they
joined together.

And then there
was light.

The light made even more dots
in colors never seen before.

And these got together
as well and formed
dots of every size.

One of these new
dots—the third one
from the sun—was
a very special
shade of blue.

The blue was
because it was covered
with water.

And when the warm,
yellow light...

mixed with the
blue water, it made
something new.

Something alive.

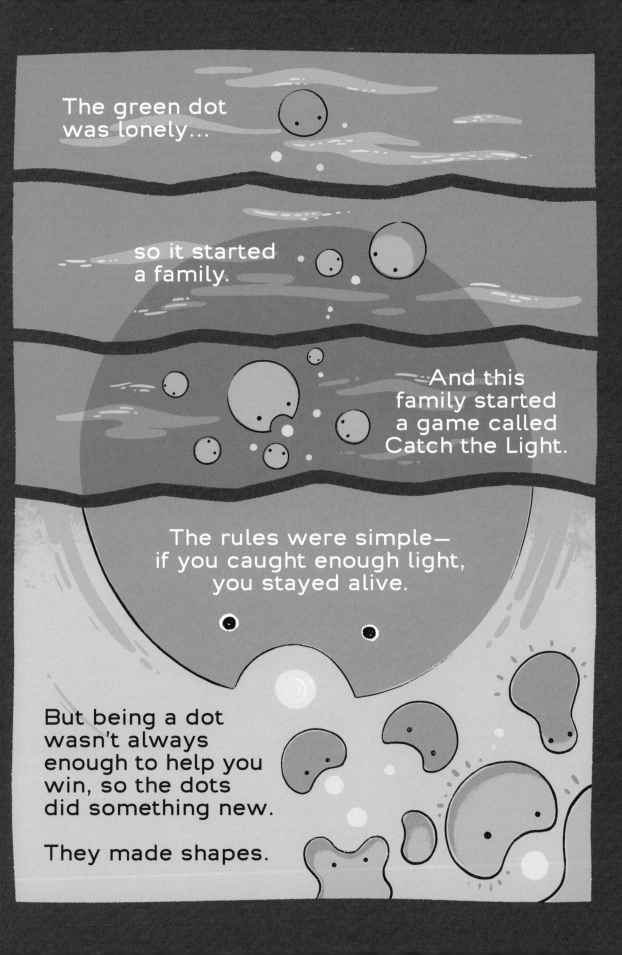

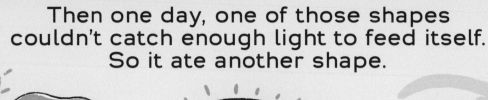

Then one day, one of those shapes
couldn't catch enough light to feed itself.
So it ate another shape.

And it got bigger
and stronger.
So it ate more.

That changed the game.
Instead of Catch the Light,
the game was now called
Eat Or Be Eaten.

Then one day,
to escape the game,
one of those creatures
climbed out of
the water.

Much bigger.

But some
got smaller.

Then one day
a dot fell out
of the sky.

A **big** dot.

When the
big dot hit
the blue dot...

...the explosion turned the whole sky red.

The world was on fire...

...and all the land-fish burned.

But one thing survived.

Remember that little fur-thing?

Her home underground kept her alive.

Some grew teeth...

and some grew claws.

Some ran
fast...

and some
climbed trees.

But one day, a fur-thing appeared that didn't have sharp teeth.

It didn't have claws.

It didn't even have a lot of warm fur.

It had something new.

A big **brain**.

So to stay alive,
it used its
big brain to
make things.

It made its
own claws.

It made its own fur.

That made
their children
even smarter.

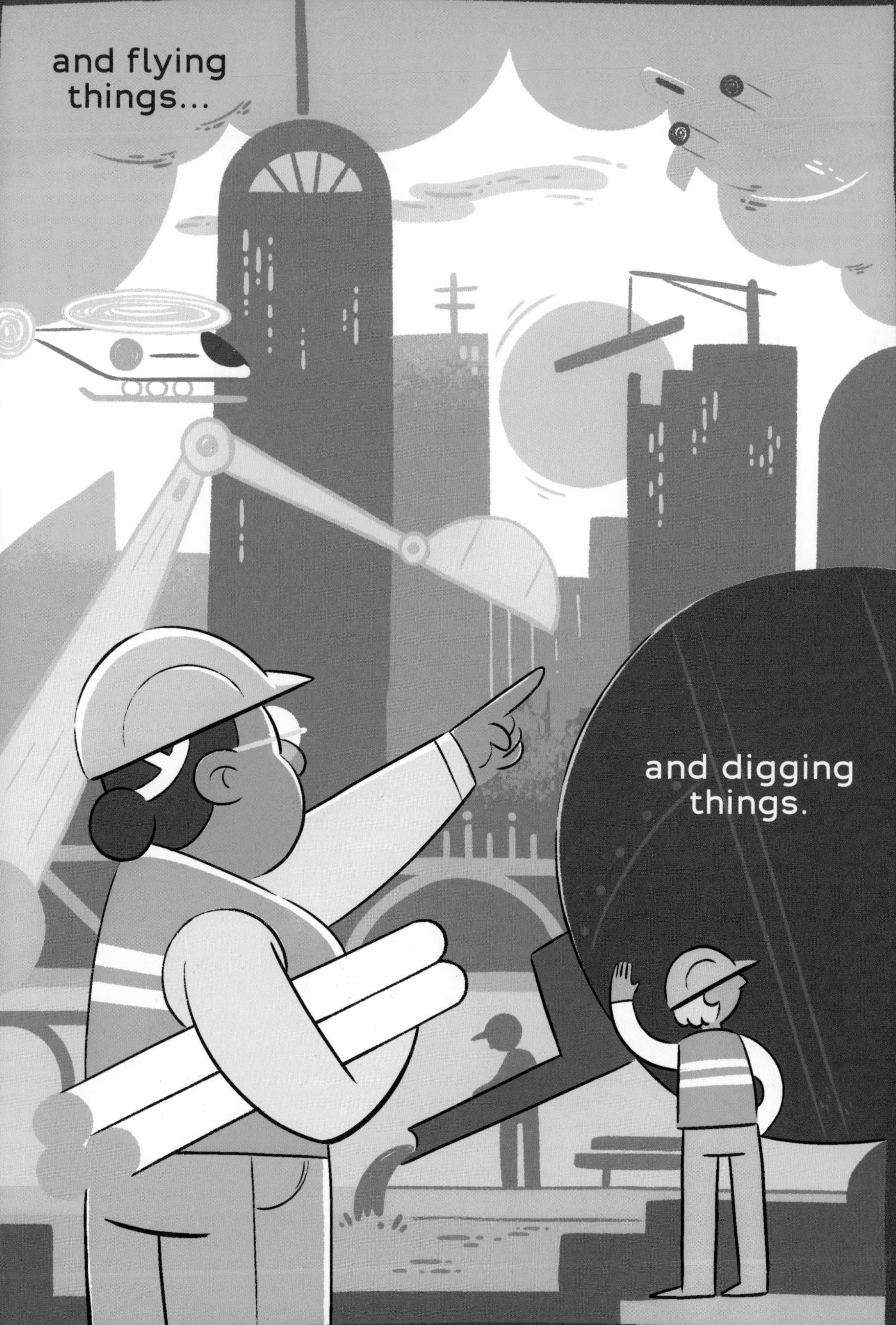
and flying things...
and digging things.

Whatever they needed to stay alive.

And just like the black dot and the green dot and the land-fish and the fur-things before them, these creatures made more of themselves.

They had families.
They had you.

These amazing creatures
could make anything and
learn everything.
But despite all that...

there was
one question
that they could
not answer...

Where did that first
dot come from?

The Big Bang
13.7 billion years ago

All matter and energy,
space and time come
into existence in a
massive explosion.

First stars form
13.5 billion years ago

Hydrogen molecules collide
at high speeds to create
the nuclear fission that
forms stars.

The Earth is born
4.5 billion years ago

The Earth forms from the
merging of stellar dust and
gas in our local solar system.

K/T Extinction Event
65 million years ago

One well-supported theory is that
a large asteroid struck the Yucatán
Peninsula in Mexico. The resulting
explosion destroyed three-quarters
of all life on Earth, including dinosaurs.

Mesozoic Era
250–66 million years ago

The Age of Reptiles, when
dinosaurs ruled the Earth.
Also known as the Age of
Conifers, ancestors of pine
trees, that served as a rich food
supply for the dinosaurs.

Miocene epoch
23.8–5 million years ago

The emergence of large
mammals such as mastodons
and glyptodons, as well as fast-
running predators and apes.

First ancestor of
Homo sapiens
2.5 million years ago

The earliest ancestors of
modern humans emerge in
Africa. The first evidence of
the use of stone tools appears.